It's Never Too Late To Find Love!

Finding Love After Failure

by Mark Dotson

Copyright © 2020, Mark E. Dotson. All Rights reserved. This book, or parts thereof, may not be reproduced in any form without permission from the publisher; exceptions are made for brief excerpts used in published reviews.

Table of Contents

Through Failure We Will Find Success	3
What Happened?	6
But Why Do We Want To Be In Love In The First Place?	10
What Am I Doing Wrong?	17
How Can I Change What I Am Doing Wrong?	20
Keep Feeding The Train's Engine!	24
Yes, It is Possible!	29

"I'm selfish, impatient and a little insecure. I make mistakes, I am out of control and at times hard to handle. But if you can't handle me at my worst, then you sure as hell don't deserve me at my best."

— **Marilyn Monroe**

Through Failure We Will Find Success

Intro

You most likely bought this book because you have almost given up hope that you will never find the love of your life or maybe the love of your life has passed on and you are left feeling empty inside and want to find that one to make you feel whole again. Whatever your reasons were to pick up a copy, there is a need in your life that is not being fulfilled and that need is to be loved and to feel significant in someone else's life that loves you once again.

As humans we all have 3 basic needs. We have the need to feel secure, loved and significant. When those needs are not being met, it feels like a part of you is missing and there is a huge hole inside of you. It is like a car that is running out of gas and you are miles away from the nearest gas station.

Empty. That is a very nagging feeling and it tends to stick with you. I know it did for me. I would see posts on Facebook where people would get engaged and think " I am not going to celebrate that with a Like" because I was envious and wondering why I cannot find such happiness. Some real and genuine happiness! Not just someone to fill your time with and leave you feeling empty. Where is that person that adds value to my life and fills me with energy and ignites that spark in my heart to get it beating once again in the rhythm of love?

So you go about your work and life busying yourself so you don't have to think about all those things. With a full mind and planner, the thoughts of being single and alone don't creep inside our mind so easily. Or worse, we engage in things that are bad for us such as alcohol or drugs that will remove the pain but only temporarily. Yeah...been there too. It didn't help. Oh it masked the pain but it created new problems to deal with. The problems of destruction of friendships, work and family. It's like looking for the answer at the bottom of every liquor or beer bottle. You never find it down there.

So now that you are fully depressed, let's also have some fun and make this a light hearted book!

I think it is wise to try and explore why all this happened in the first place and take a snapshot view of the situation. As a Mechanic by trade, my job is to do a visual inspection, verify the problem, perform a diagnosis, replace or repair parts and then test the machine to verify that the problem is resolved.

Those things apply whether you are working on an engine or working on a relationship...well...with the exception of replacing the parts!

"To love at all is to be vulnerable. Love anything and your heart will be wrung and possibly broken. If you want to make sure of keeping it intact you must give it to no one, not even an animal. Wrap it carefully round with hobbies and little luxuries; avoid all entanglements. Lock it up safe in the casket or coffin of your selfishness. But in that casket, safe, dark, motionless, airless, it will change. It will not be broken; it will become unbreakable, impenetrable, irredeemable. To love is to be vulnerable."

— **C.S. Lewis**

What Happened?

In order to fix something, you have to know what is broken...

My love life was a train wreck from the word GO. So many things that went wrong and so many bad decisions along the way led me to believe that maybe I would never find the real love or the soul mate that had always eluded me.

Here I was with 3 failed marriages and a carnage of train wreck relationships left in the wake. It wasn't until I started to understand myself that things began to make sense and why those train wrecks occurred in the first place. And it wasn't until I left all the negativity behind that prevented the positive things from happening, did things begin to turn around. You do not attract the love of your life with a negative attitude towards love. It makes people walk or run the other way.

When things start going south, we often see it worse than it is. Oh she is going to leave me or we are going to break up. This creates fear in us and causes us to pull back. We stop sending those funny or romantic texts. We stop taking or block their phone call or stop talking in person. We avoid each other and avoid doing anything that will trigger your partner. Finally enough is enough and then we separate. Done, finished and over. NEXT! And the pattern continues over and over and will so unless you interrupt it.

So many things can invade and destroy your relationships. For me, it is was being selfish and not continuing to do the things I did in the first place to attract the person I wanted. Then the communication would breakdown and the rest was history and so was I. As I look back now, it was stupid but in my particular case there were some extenuating circumstances and we all have them. We are all prisoners of our past at some point and mine was a war that left me with PTSD. I don't want to use that as an excuse, I just want you to know that many things can intervene in our relationships from our past experiences.

There are a 1,000 things that can happen in a relationship to cause problems. In today's world it is often technology. That innocent text can turn into a long lasting affair or adding that person on Facebook that you are attracted to can open the door to trouble. Everyone is trying to escape their problems and hoping that by being with you their problems would magically disappear. Unfortunately the world does not work like that. So then we try another and another and another and end up with the same results. Why? Because we are falling into the same pattern and cycle. We start out all excited and romantic and then it loses its luster and then we sabotage the relationship. Well, at least that is how it would work for me and the trail of train wrecks kept piling up.

Again, we so often let the past invade our minds and screw things up. My PTSD would cause me to self-medicate with booze or drugs when my life spiraled out of control. The spouse or girlfriend that was in my life at the time because I didn't do booze or drugs would get sideways with me and the problems began with self-medicating. But I didn't really start to figure that out until I was clinically diagnosed with PTSD and basically verified that I was "crazy". So now I have something to work with! You know the mechanic in me said "We just verified the problem". That is of course after we blame the other person for being crazy and sometimes they are.

It took me a long time to realize that I needed to be mentally ready for the right relationship. I had to give up the selfishness, be more kind hearted and be more willing to listen with empathy. It didn't mean that I was any less of a man, it meant that I was being a better man and what a difference that made in the relationship! It was like night and day!

So now is a good time for you to do some real soul searching and ask yourself "what happened?" Put away all the "it was all their fault" thinking and take a look inside of you at your faults. They are there if you really look hard enough. As I mentioned, I was selfish and sometimes not very kind hearted...especially when they did something to make me angry. PTSD can have a tendency to make you angry at things that you shouldn't be angry about. I had to get a handle on those things in order to ensure that I would be mentally ready for a relationship. That is also an ongoing process that one needs to keep working on themselves to be better at.

The only person you need to be better than is the person you were yesterday.

"Darkness cannot drive out darkness: only light can do that. Hate cannot drive out hate: only love can do that."

— **Martin Luther King Jr.**

But Why Do We Want To Be In Love In The First Place?

Being in love provides something that is missing in our lives. It is that spark in your heart that makes you feel fully alive. You wake up in the morning with a new attitude that makes you want to reach for the stars and dig into your work. That special person in your life flashes through your mind during the day and gives you a reason to get up each day and live life to the fullest.

Love is the greatest thing on this earth. In fact, the Bible teaches us "And now these three remain: faith, hope and love. But the greatest of these is love." We love our kids, our family and friends and we want to be invested in love with our significant other to complete the circle and the memories that come along with it. Love inspires us to be more and do more and it adds passion to our lives. Love is kind and is not self seeking and I think a hard one for many of us is that love is patient. In a fast paced world, patience is often not to be found.

When you don't have that little spark in your heart, you may feel depressed, lonely or just wanting to end it all. You feel as if you are not worthy of anyone's love and that you have failed yourself. Those are perfectly normal emotions to feel and I have felt them all myself. They can be as debilitating as they can be. But those emotions can also used to help propel you towards your hearts desires. Use your pain to propel you forward!

Love is a great feeling in the beginning but as time marches on, it may begin to lose that spark that attracted you in the first place. That is one of the problems I had in relationships. I am a Type A personality and would all of a sudden have this huge rush of falling in love and then as the newness of it wore off, I would begin to lose interest. I failed to realize that love is a verb and continue the actions that made it special and real.

I think a better question is "Why wouldn't you want to be in love?" Sharing your life with someone and all the experiences in it are what we are here for. We are not meant to live solitary empty lives. We are meant to live our lives full of joy and that joy comes from love.

True love can open the doors to so much happiness and joy. When two people are 100% invested in making the relationship work and continuing to work at making their love grow, it can be a magical thing. Being single can be like going on a vacation alone. You have nobody to share the ride with and experience the things you are doing and seeing. Sure, it can be fun by yourself, but it is much more enjoyable with someone else. That being said, you must be comfortable being single and living alone. If you just want a relationship to have someone there, you are sacrificing your insecurity of being lonely for your chance at real love.

I know for me, there were so many things that I have done and seen alone and when you try to explain them to someone, they don't fully get it. They would have if they would if they were there with you along for the ride.

We all have a craving for the human connection. Some of us are more solitary by nature and some of us need an intense close relationship. This is an important thing to know about yourself because if you are more solitary by nature and end up with someone who needs an intense closeness, there are going to be problems. Real problems that will have to be dealt with sooner than later.

So as you can see, humans need the human connection. They need love, security and the need to feel significant by someone that cares and loves them.

Lust Is Not Love

She Blinded Me With Science!

Have you ever heard the song "Looking for love in all the wrong places?" If so, you have a pretty good idea about what lust is about and that it is just about looking for a partner.

Lust is the desire for sexual gratification. BUT, it is my belief that you must have some lust for the person you are seeking because that means you are physically attracted to them.

Without getting too technical, I want to delve into how our chemistry assists with these different feelings of Lust, Attraction and Attachment.

Lust

The hypothalamus part of your brain helps stimulate the release of two chemicals associated with lust. Those chemicals are the sexual hormones Testosterone and Estrogen. Men have Testosterone and the ladies have Estrogen. I am sure you have seen a TV Ad that sells products to increase Testosterone. When that Testosterone level is lowered as a man ages, his sex drive decreases. He may seem to not be as sexually active because of a lack of a chemical in his body.

And I might add that Testosterone and Estrogen can literally make the brain "high" for a week or more. It is an incredible high that seems to last forever and makes you full of life and empowers you to be better at everything. When you "come down", it can leave you with a feeling of emptiness and then you want to replenish this feeling much like a drunk wants to have another drink. It is an intoxicating feeling no doubt about it, but it is short lived.

Lust can fool you into thinking that it is really love. You find someone that is attractive and seems to fill all of your requirements and you become intimate with one another.

This might go on for some time and you think everything is just wonderful. Mr. or Mrs Right is working out and you have found the love of your life.

But one day it will begin to dawn on you and you begin to realize that your heart is not aligned with this person and soon regret will set in.

It can be hard to determine if your relationship is based on love or lust. Why? Because you have to totally separate the two for the answer to reveal itself. This means you have to separate your heart from the lust feeling. When you are with this person, are you thinking about doing things for them to make them feel loved or are you thinking only about sexual desires? You must follow your heart, but listen to your gut. Your gut is never wrong but your heart often is.

If you really want to test this theory, tell the other person that you want to abstain from anything sexual and then see how long you stay together. It will reveal itself pretty quickly. It could be quite shocking and can also end in pain of a breakup in the relationship. But, you are on your search for love and not lust.

When you find that true love/heart connection, making love will be the ultimate expression of love between you both. Anything else is just a false sense of love and that is never going to fulfill your desire to have your heart intertwined with someone else.

Lust is a very powerful thing because we all have a need for intimacy and we think that if we are intimate, we must be in love with each other. The feelings are there but it can be that the testosterone and estrogen are fooling us into thinking that this is real and lasting love.

Attraction

An attraction to someone rewards the brain when you feel attracted to a person. Through doses of Dopamine and Nor epinephrine released from the brain, it provides a sort of chemical reward that lets us know we have an attraction to them.

Dopamine is released when we are doing things that we enjoy. Sex and spending time with family and friends are common things that trigger the release.

These two chemicals can make us full of energy and euphoric and can lead to suppressed appetite and insomnia.

Attraction can also lead to a reduction of Serotonin which is thought to be a chemical that involves infatuation and the beginning stages of love.

Attachment

When you have a long-term relationship, attachment is a necessary component. Attachment forms the deep bonds and friendship, social cordiality and other intimate functions of the relationship.

There are chemicals that support attachment as they do in attraction and lust. These are Oxytocin and Vasopressin.

You can receive a dose of Oxytocin when you cuddle or hug one another. This is one of the reasons we feel good after we hug someone.

Vasopressin is a normally occurring hormone that helps control normal body functions.

Both men and women naturally produce vasopressin, yet men experience its effects more strongly because of how it interacts with the male sex hormone Testosterone.

So as you can see, certain chemicals provide different responses to the brain and the effects vary widely. This makes it a bit tricky when we are thinking that "this is the one" during our romance and dating rituals.

"People think a soul mate is your perfect fit, and that's what everyone wants. But a true soul mate is a mirror, the person who shows you everything that is holding you back, the person who brings you to your own attention so you can change your life.

A true soul mate is probably the most important person you'll ever meet, because they tear down your walls and smack you awake. But to live with a soul mate forever? Nah. Too painful. Soul mates, they come into your life just to reveal another layer of yourself to you, and then leave.

A soul mates purpose is to shake you up, tear apart your ego a little bit, show you your obstacles and addictions, break your heart open so new light can get in, make you so desperate and out of control that you have to transform your life, then introduce you to your spiritual master..."

— Elizabeth Gilbert

What Am I Doing Wrong?

Now isn't that the question that keeps running through your mind! What am I doing wrong? What is wrong with me? Why don't they love me? Why did they leave me?

Questions are the answers. When we ask ourselves better questions, we will have better outcomes from those questions.

It could be that you are doing NOTHING wrong. The other person many not be mentally ready for the relationship, so don't just assume that it is YOU!

This is the time for great introspection and to look at the events that led up to your past relationships ending. As you get older, things become more clear about what you want and don't what in your life. I call these the non-negotiables. For example, I do not want a relationship with a drug addict or an alcoholic. These are not negotiable at all. There is no "OK, I will go out with you if you quit using drugs or stop drinking". It is just something that I want no part of in my life. Period.

As you are thinking about how those relationships ended, ask yourself if it was something that you did that made it end? Were you in the best mental or physical state to be in that relationship? Was it someone that you were compatible with or were you just "settling" because someone finally said yes?

This introspection should go quite deep within you and you need to be looking at all areas of your life. For example, I am a neat, clean and organized person and someone who is not the same is not attractive to me. They could be the best looking person on the planet but live in chaos and filth and that is a BIG turn off to me.

You have to remember that now you are preparing yourself to be the best person you can be to attract the best person to your life. Positive actions attract positive people. Who wants to hang around someone that is dull and negative all the time? Nope!

Did the other person try to change you in any way? This can be a big red flag. If they are wanting you to change to make your life better such as not eating bad foods, then they may have been looking out for your best interests and showing you that they care. But, if they start controlling who your friends are or where you go, then that was a sign of a bad relationship developing. Controlling people are just manipulators and the world is full of them. This is fed by their insecurities and fears. Don't feed into that.

It is hard to be completely honest with ourselves because we are quick to blame the other person for it not working out. Just look at our divorce system today and the fighting over money, the kids, the house, the dog and the cat.

Was there abuse either physical or mental in the relationship? Either of those is not OK and should never be tolerated. Men can just as easily be abused as women. They may not receive as much physical abuse but the mental abuse can certainly happen.

I saved the big one for last and that is communication. Did you effectively communicate in a loving and non-threatening manner? Or did you scream and shout at each other at the top of your lungs? Good effective communication is THE most important part of a loving and growing relationship. If you are not good at it, start learning how to be good at it. Go to YouTube and watch some videos or read some books on effective listening and communicating. It will not only help you in relationships, but it will help you in your work life too.

Good communication is also important for couples that need mental stimulation in a relationship. Let's face it, making love is only about 1% of your time together, so the other 99% of the time better be spent doing things together creating memories and having wonderful and stimulating conversation that you never tire of. I like to use the term "making mental love" to your partner when I think of how deep that connection can be.

The Past

This is probably the biggest relationship killer of all! People want to drag their tent along and set it up and camp out there. You don't live in the past anymore but you feel the need to bring it up to your partner to try and help heal yourself. DON'T! Let's say you were a victim of sexual abuse and you were to describe in detail how these things happened to you. Now while you are making love with your partner, those mental images are stuck in their head. BOOM....it's done and over with. There are people that you can share your past with such as a Pastor, your best friend, a psychologist, therapist or anyone else in your circle of trust. But don't be bringing that into a healthy relationship unless you want to sabotage it.

They say opposites attract, but I believe that is only on the North and South poles of magnets. Yes, you can bring things to the table that help balance out a relationship and that is a great thing. But if they have too many differences, it can open a whole new set of problems that will eventually have to be dealt with. Finding someone with common life experiences and tastes makes for a great friendship that can turn into a wonderful relationship.

How Can I Change What I Am Doing Wrong?

Change begins with you. In order to change your life, you have to change your habits and actions. Change can be a difficult thing because you have been doing the same habits over and over for many years. Habits are difficult to break depending on which habit it is. Change your habits and you will change your life.

As you looked back at your cycle of train wreck relationships, did you notice any patterns that emerged? Mine were selfishness and that was a habit that I needed to break and become more humble and less proud. I needed to be less negative and stop letting the negativity of the world creep into my mind and then I regurgitated it to others. I needed to be more positive and worry less. I needed to be more kind and less arrogant. I....you see how all of this comes down to I? I need to.....

You must start changing those things which caused you to fail. I had a bad habit of sabotaging the relationship. When things were going great and it was getting more serious, that meant I would have to take this relationship more seriously and be fully committed. That caused fear to creep inside of me and I would start doing things like pulling away, not answering calls or texts etc. This was not good and made the other person guess because the communication had broken down as well. I was letting the fear from my past train wreck relationships destroy my present and future ones. We sabotage in other areas of our lives too such as work and friendships.

I once met a Dentist who had a wife that left him. He was devastated. He let his life spiral out of control because he was paralyzed with fear and eventually he lost his Dental practice. He linked his belief system of a failed marriage to him being a failure. I was doing the same thing. I linked love to equal pain and marriage to equal divorce. Until someone came into my life that showed me that this is all BS, I may still be linking those emotions to pain. Yes, it can be painful, but it doesn't have to last a lifetime. You have already paid the price so stop writing new checks to pay for your old mistakes.

You don't have to try and change everything at one time. Baby steps. Take one thing in your life and change how you are doing it. Are you an alcoholic? Start by drinking less or if possible, give it up for good. The things we put into our bodies do nothing more than to change our state. We want to be happy, we drink or use drugs. We want to calm down, we smoke a cigarette. Each chemical we use alters our state. Your coffee in the morning uses caffeine to jumpstart your day. For me, it is tea. I guess I figure if I have given up all my other bad habits, I am not giving up the tea! But my drinking tea is not going to end a relationship.

Making small changes and taking small steps can produce some incredible results. A slight turn of the rudder on an airplane changes its course. You must continually provide inputs to the rudder over a long flight to reach your destination. The rudder controls the direction the plane is headed and your internal rudder should alter your destination to find that real and lasting love you long for.

Make a list of those things you need to work on. Lists make us more accountable over time. The most beautiful thing about life is that we can change our habits immediately! A big ship takes a long time to turn around but you can turn around on a dime. Find those areas that you know will have the greatest impact for change and get started by changing them!

The law of attraction states that you get back what you send out. What are you sending out? Are you a happy or sad person? Are you playing the victim to create an excuse or get attention for what is happening in your relationships?

We all can make excuses for not to move ahead and change. I can't lose that weight. I can't stop drinking. I can't exercise because I have no time. You must turn those I cant's into I cans. You have the greatest reward in the world coming to you when you make those changes to attract someone wonderful into your life! But try to chose someone that is an equal amount of "crazy" as you. Yes, we all have a little crazy inside of us!

An accountability partner is a great way to ensure that you are making those changes in your life. But you must pick a strong person that will be completely honest with you and will have the strength to hold you accountable. Being an accountability partner requires a lot of discipline to follow through and do the things required. Choose wisely.

Live, learn and love.

"I no longer believed in the idea of soul mates, or love at first sight. But I was beginning to believe that a very few times in your life, if you were lucky, you might meet someone who was exactly right for you. Not because he was perfect, or because you were, but because your combined flaws were arranged in a way that allowed two separate beings to hinge together."

— **Lisa Kleypas**

Keep Feeding The Train's Engine!

It is kind of like the old steam trains that required coal to fire their engines. You must keep feeding the coal to that engine to heat the water that creates the steam to make the engine work to move the train. When I stopped putting the coal in the engine, the train slowed down and eventually stopped dead in its tracks. Or it is the airplane that suddenly runs out of fuel and falls from the sky. I think you get the picture.

It is not easy to keep the spark ignited, but you have to go back to the simple things that made the difference before. Time and kindness go a long way to get you back down the tracks. What we do is stop doing the little things that kept the relationship fun and alive. It's the stuff we need to do while we have a thousand other things running through our brains and when we are overwhelmed, we jettison something. That something is usually those little things.

Or your partner does something and it makes you angry. It's easy to get selfish and then just cut them off from everything. You know...that payback routine. We have all been there.

So what are you actually going to do? You are going to have to fulfill those needs of security, safety and significance.

Words

Choose wisely. Words can be sharp as a knife and once you say them, they cannot be taken back. Your words need to be kind and convey a sense of security and protection of the relationship.

Your words can also have a great impact and be one of the small things you do. Words like "goodnight baby or good morning baby" start someone's day off right. Find out what your partner likes to be called that makes them feel significant. Most people just chose something and the other person interprets it the wrong way...so ask!

Words whispered at the right time can also be wonderful to hear. This secret communication is tantalizing and peaks your interest. Your words are what attracted that mental part of your relationship in the beginning and should be never ending. Words have the power to heal or destroy and that is why we must use them wisely. We all wish we would have decided to use our words better at different times and regret that, but that is all behind you now.

Before you speak, ask yourself if the words you are going to use are kind and gentle or do they invoke anger? Do they build the person up or break them down?

Actions

Don't move so fast in the relationship that it scares the other person and pushes them away. Remember, they may not have a great track record either, so let the relationship proceed with a sense of slowness. This is a time to get to know one another and ask questions to get to know them more deeply. Rushing anything normally ends in disaster. Haste makes waste.

Note: **Dating is a process to see if you are compatible with each other. Too often we skip right through that to intimacy and the train goes off the rails rather quickly.**

Make sure your partner knows where they stand in the relationship by telling them and showing them. All the words spoken mean nothing if there is no action to back them up.

It's Never Too Late to Find Love

Love is a feeling but love is also a verb, an action. It takes action to find love and to maintain that love.

What is your plan of action? If you fail to plan, you plan to fail.

Plan - to be a better person

Plan - to be a kinder person

Pan - to be a more sincere person

Plan - to back up your words with actions

<u>Here is an idea for your "Plan"</u>

   Plan to love unconditionally

   Listen with empathy and love

   Always put their needs and wants before your own

   Never put them down, only build them up

The little things are the big things. I like romance and was thinking that I want more of that in my life. Romance is not the big things like an expensive trip to some far away destination. Romance can be simple things like cooking dinner together and enjoying it over a candlelit dinner. Yes!

The little things can also seem mundane like doing the laundry, making the bed, washing the dishes, cleaning the house or car, but, these are also the things that prove through action that you do care and help prove your love. One person doing all of these all the time can create a rift in the relationship that will only grow.

How about leaving a sticky note where it will be found with a message such as "I believe in you"? Send a romantic text. Search the web for a thousand more...but don't overdo it. There has to be a balance in everything you do. Overdoing it makes you seem clingy or needy. Yes, you are seeking to fill your need for significance in someone's life, but there is a limit.

There is a limit to everything before you go overboard. This is where great communication skills come in. You have to be in a position to talk to your partner with no fear of retribution. That is when you can have the most meaningful conversations of your lives. You must allow yourself to be vulnerable to be loved.

If you are a laid back person with a Type A personality, there could be some friction there. If you can find the balance to keep feeding that fire, that is a wonderful thing. It takes a lot more give and take in a relationship like that but that does not mean that it will not work.

"Love is like the wind, you can't see it but you can feel it."

— **Nicholas Sparks**

Yes, It is Possible!

We always save the best for last and this holds true for this last chapter. Yes, it is possible to find the true love that we have always wanted to have. I live in a pretty remote area so it makes things a little more difficult, but that doesn't mean that the love you find will be right next door. It could be across town or across the country and with things like Internet dating websites and Facebook, you never know where romance will come from.

You may have read the words "I don't want to be your first love, I want to be your last love". I can think of no better way to describe what you want out of your love life. To be their last love and to create the memories that they will take with them to the end of their days. It sounds romantic because it is romantic. You are at an age that the game playing is not in your dictionary and being able to be open and honest are things that you live by. At this point we all have more time in the rearview mirror than we do in the windshield, so you don't have time to waste on something that is not worth your time.

You must never give up hope that you can find your true love. But, you must also go out and find it. "Seek and ye shall find", "knock and it will be opened unto you" are some words of wisdom straight out of the Bible and they hold a lot of truth. Your true love is not going to come knock on your door, well unless they are the Amazon, UPS or FedEx driver. Chances of that.... ah...not so good.

It is when we give up hope that we give up our chances. Get out and live your life and meet new people. This is a hard one for me as I am very much at home in the cabin and can hole up for long periods of time without seeing another human being. But I found that I need to get out because it is not healthy for us to not have some human interaction from time to time.

Go to your local church to be with community. You can also volunteer at local events as that is a great way to meet people. The bar scene is way behind me. Not that there aren't good people in bars, but there are a lot of problems associated with that as well. There are much better places to search for your soul mate.

One thing that has changed my entire world is becoming a more positive person and putting out positive actions. The entire group of people that I surround myself with now are like night and day different. But that is what you must do is change yourself. So often we try to change the other person and you never want to do that. They are who they are and changing them to suit your needs will never work. If they are self-destructing, then helping them change some bad habits such as drug abuse is a different story.

A lot of this book comes down to believing that things are possible. I once heard Zig Ziglar say "If I was down to my last 2 dollars, I would go buy a money belt!" There is a ton of truth in that statement. If you do not believe in something, you will not make a concerted effort to make it work. A half-hearted attempt at something usually results in little to no success.

One thing that you must remember is that anything in this life worth having takes work and love is no exception. It takes work to find the person, to fall in love with the person, dating and just every day interactions. Yes, love should come naturally, but doing the things that prove that love take work. Like making dinner, making a gift for them, driving across the state to see them and other acts that prove that love. Stephen Covey says "love is a verb, love is action." Yes it is!

You can say you love someone but it is all proven out by your actions.

A wise man asked me one day what the definition of love was and I didn't have much of an answer. He said "love is when you put the needs and wants of someone else before your own." I don't think you can sum it up much better than that. Love is a verb and by sacrificing your own needs for someone else's proves it to be true.

With a plan to go out and seek what your heart has been searching for, you will be much more likely to succeed at finding it. It is out there, you just have to continue to search until you find it.

I wish you the best on your journey to find happiness and love!

    Never give up, never give in and never give out!

"Only once in your life, I truly believe, you find someone who can completely turn your world around. You tell them things that you've never shared with another soul and they absorb everything you say and actually want to hear more. You share hopes for the future, dreams that will never come true, goals that were never achieved and the many disappointments life has thrown at you. When something wonderful happens, you can't wait to tell them about it, knowing they will share in your excitement. They are not embarrassed to cry with you when you are hurting or laugh with you when you make a fool of yourself. Never do they hurt your feelings or make you feel like you are not good enough, but rather they build you up and show you the things about yourself that make you special and even beautiful. There is never any pressure, jealousy or competition but only a quiet calmness when they are around. You can be yourself and not worry about what they will think of you because they love you for who you are. The things that seem insignificant to most people such as a note, song or walk become invaluable treasures kept safe in your heart to cherish forever. Memories of your childhood come back and are so clear and vivid it's like being young again. Colours seem brighter and more brilliant. Laughter seems part of

daily life where before it was infrequent or didn't exist at all. A phone call or two during the day helps to get you through a long day's work and always brings a smile to your face. In their presence, there's no need for continuous conversation, but you find you're quite content in just having them nearby. Things that never interested you before become fascinating because you know they are important to this person who is so special to you. You think of this person on every occasion and in everything you do. Simple things bring them to mind like a pale blue sky, gentle wind or even a storm cloud on the horizon. You open your heart knowing that there's a chance it may be broken one day and in opening your heart, you experience a love and joy that you never dreamed possible. You find that being vulnerable is the only way to allow your heart to feel true pleasure that's so real it scares you. You find strength in knowing you have a true friend and possibly a soul mate who will remain loyal to the end. Life seems completely different, exciting and worthwhile. Your only hope and security is in knowing that they are a part of your life."

— **Bob Marley**

And now it's your turn to get out there and turn your dreams into reality. The world awaits you and so does that special someone that you would rather live with than live without.

We are all looking for that soul mate, not a cell mate. There is a very distinct difference and I don't want you to be settling for anyone that doesn't help make you a better person and propel you forward. Life is just too short for that. Let's do this!

I want to personally thank you for reading this book. It took a lot of soul searching for me to make myself vulnerable and expose my train wreck relationships. But, I learned a great deal about myself through it and I suggest you put your life to pen and paper and you will learn more about yourself too.

Your kindness would be appreciated in a review of this book on Amazon or wherever you purchased it.

Thank you once again for sharing a little of my life with you.

Sincerely,

Mark E. Dotson

Another book I wrote that you may be interested in to help guide you through some struggles of life is: **<u>Cutting Through the Chaos of Making a Life & a Living</u>**.

Getting from where you are to where you want to be can be a daunting task. There are many twists and turns, uphills and downhills in this thing called "life" and the choices we make can either make or break us.

We all make choices both good and bad. Your ability to navigate these choices to determine which are best for you is one of the most important things you can do to secure a great future.

This book includes practical tools and interactive questions that you can apply to your life to help steer you in the right direction.

Ride along on a journey that I have taken that will help guide and inspire you to make your way through this thing called "life".

You don't need to live your life like a "sailboat without a rudder." Together we will sail off into the sunset and start a new life in a new direction.

Buckle up, it's going to be a fun ride ahead!

Mark E. Dotson

"The choices you make…can have an impact for a lifetime."

Cutting Through The Chaos of Making a Life & a Living

Mark E. Dotson

CPSIA information can be obtained
at www.ICGtesting.com
Printed in the USA
LVHW091046220322
714090LV00004B/83